OXFORD
UNIVERSITY PRESS

Sport

Then and Now

Shilo Berry

Contents

Introduction

Some sports have been played for hundreds of years. Some of these sports have changed a lot. The rules have changed. The clothes have changed. The **equipment** has changed.

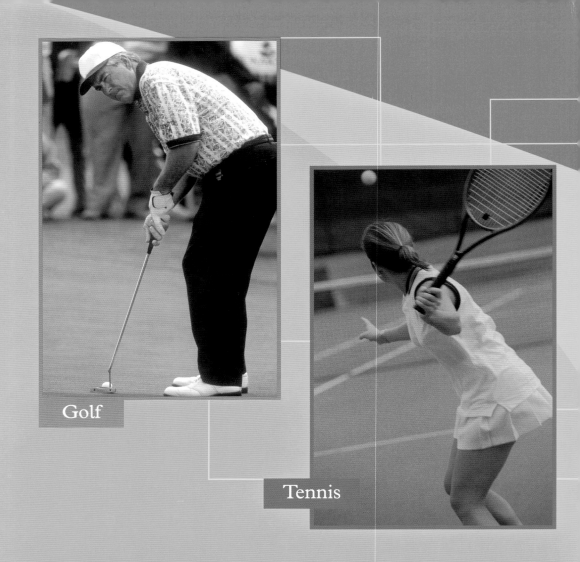

Golf

Tennis

This book looks at five different sports. These sports are golf, tennis, swimming, rugby and cricket.

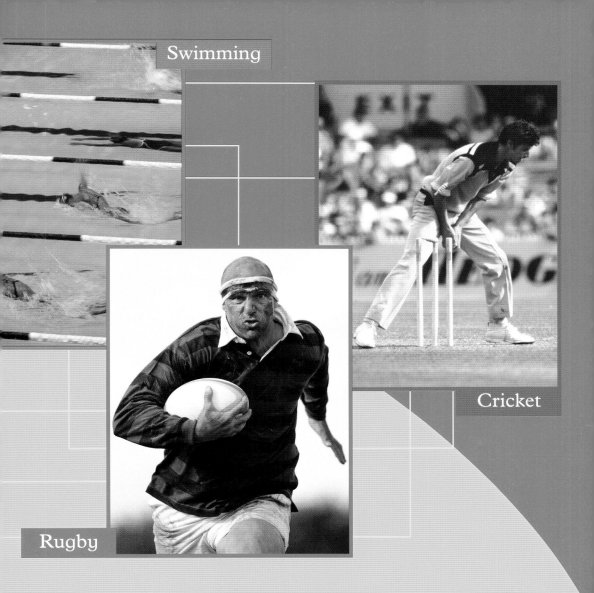

Swimming

Cricket

Rugby

It looks at the changes in clothes worn to play each sport. It looks at the changes in **equipment** used to play each sport.

Golf

When people first played golf, they wore very formal clothes. They wore long trousers and skirts. They wore formal hats and shoes.

Then

6

Now

hat

shirt

golf glove

trousers

golf shoes

Today, people wear more casual clothes. They wear trousers and shirts, or even shorts and T-shirts. They also wear special golf shoes. Golf shoes have thin spikes on the bottom. The spikes stop the golfers' feet from slipping. Today, golfers wear a golf glove on one hand so that they can grip the golf club when it is wet.

Then

Now

golf-club shaft

golf-club head

Golf clubs today look much the same as they did in the past, but they are made of new **materials**. In the past, golf clubs were made of wood. Today, most golf clubs are made of different metals.

Materials Golf Equipment Is Made From

Date	Golf-Club Head	Golf-Club Shaft	Golf Ball
1600	wood	wood	wood
1820	wood or metal	wood	feathers wrapped in leather
1940	wood or light metal	strong metal	rubber
2000	light metal	strong new material	rubber and plastic

Golf balls today also look much the same as they did in the past. However, they, too, are made of new **materials**. The first golf balls were made of wood. After that balls were made of feathers tightly wrapped in leather. Golf balls today are made from rubber covered with plastic.

Tennis

Women's tennis clothes have changed a lot over the years. In the early 1900s, women had to wear white clothes. Tennis skirts were long. The first short skirt was worn in 1922. It was not very short!

Then

Now

Tennis player in short skirt

Tennis player in short skirt and coloured T-shirt

Today, tennis skirts are very short. They are close-fitting. Players can wear coloured clothes in most **tournaments**.

Old wooden rackets

Tennis rackets today still look like rackets of the past. However, they are made from different **materials**. Tennis rackets in the past were made of wood. They had strings made of animal gut. In the 1920s, leather grips were added.

People started to use rackets made of a light metal in the 1970s.

Many **materials** are used to make the tennis rackets today. These materials make the rackets lighter and stronger.

Tennis racket of today

Swimming

There have been many changes in swimming costumes over the years. In the past, costumes were made of thick, heavy wool. Men wore swimming costumes that covered their chests.

Then

Men used to wear thick woollen swimming costumes.

Today, swimming costumes are made from thin, light fabrics. Some of these fabrics are stretchy. Men wear short swimming costumes.

Some swimmers wear a tight-fitting suit that covers them from the ankles to the shoulders. It is thought that this helps the swimmer swim faster.

Now

Rugby

Jerseys worn for rugby have changed over the years. In the past, they were made of cotton. The cotton got very heavy when it was wet.

Today, jerseys are made of stretchy fabric, which is very light. It also does not get heavy when it is wet.

Now

Then

Then

Now

Over the years, rugby balls have been made out of many things. Often, the balls were made out of cowhide. Balls were also made out of pig skin and camel skin. They were both too slippery.

In the past, the ball was nearly round. Today, the ball is oval.

Cricket

Cricket is a game that has been played for many years. A long time ago cricket was played using clubs or sticks. People used a stone for a cricket ball.

Bats that look like the bats people use today were not used until about 1853. The blade of these bats was made of willow. The handle was made of cane. The cane was covered with rubber strips and tied with **twine**. All the best cricket bats today are still made of willow.

blade

handle

Then ▶

Willow cricket bat, with red ball

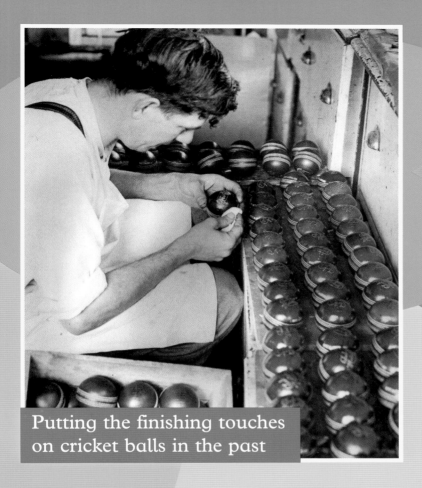

Putting the finishing touches on cricket balls in the past

Cricket balls are now made of cork. They are covered with four pieces of hand-stitched leather. They are red or white.

Formal **spectators**

The first cricket matches were played in England. The players wore formal clothes. The clothes were white. They wore top hats.

The people watching the game also wore formal clothes.

Today, the clothes players wear are not as formal. Cricket players can wear coloured clothes in some matches. The player batting can wear a helmet to protect his or her head.

Now

You can see that in each sport things have changed. New clothes are closer fitting and lighter. This helps people move faster.

New **equipment** is lighter and stronger. This helps people hit further.

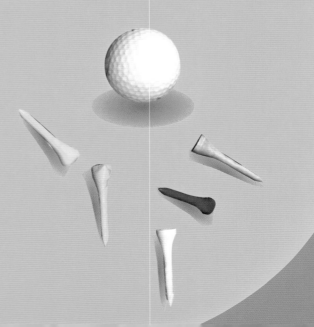

Glossary

equipment – The items or objects needed for a sport or game.

materials – What things are made of.

spectators – People who go to watch sport.

tournaments – Sports competition played by people competing for a prize.

twine – Strong string or thread.

Index